Turnip

Recipes

D1340911

Introduction

Fruits and vegetables are vital in our daily diet. Turnips are a delicious vegetable which can be cooked or raw and lend themselves to a variety of preparations.

They are delicious roasted, which is a process that mellows and yet concentrates their watery flavor at the same time.

They can also be mashed, baked, or added to soups or stews.

This cookbook contains a wide variety of delicious turnip recipes.

Scottish Clapshot

Ingredients:

1 pound baking potatoes, peeled and cubed
¾ pound turnips, peeled and cubed
¼ pound carrots, peeled and cubed
1 tsp. salt
2 tbsps. butter, cubed
3 tbsps. heavy cream

Directions:

1. Place the potatoes, turnips, carrots, and salt in a Dutch oven, fill with water to cover the vegetables and bring to a boil over high heat.
2. Reduce the heat to medium-high and boil the vegetables until tender, 20 to 25 minutes.
3. Drain and mash the vegetables with a potato masher. Spoon the mashed vegetables into a serving dish, top with cubes of butter and drizzle with cream.

Bacon Clapshot

Ingredients:

1?1/3 pounds potato, peeled and quartered
? pound turnips, peeled and cut into chunks
3 tbsps. butter
¼ cup milk
8 strips bacon, cooked and crumbled
1 pinch ground nutmeg
1 pinch salt and ground black pepper to taste

Directions:

1. Place the potatoes and turnips in a large saucepan, cover with water and bring to a boil.
2. Cook until tender, about 20 minutes.
3. Drain the potatoes and turnips, return them to the saucepan and mash until creamy.
4. Add the butter and milk and beat until fluffy.
5. Stir in the crumbled bacon and season with nutmeg, salt, and pepper.

Caramelized Turnips

Ingredients:

3 cups diced peeled turnips
¼ cup water
1 cube chicken bouillon
1 tbsp. butter, or more as needed
2 tbsps. white sugar

Directions:

1. Place the turnips into a skillet with the water and chicken bouillon cube over medium heat, and simmer until the water has evaporated and the turnips are tender, about 15 minutes.
2. Stir in the butter, let melt, and sprinkle on the sugar. Gently cook and stir the turnips until the butter and sugar cook into a brown, sticky coating on the turnips, about 10 minutes. Serve hot.

Creamy Homestyle Turnips

Ingredients:

2 tbsps. butter
3 cloves garlic, minced
5 large turnips, cut into cubes
¾ cup heavy whipping cream
½ cup grated Parmesan cheese
1 green onion, minced
½ tsp. oregano
½ tsp. parsley flakes
1 pinch salt to taste
1 pinch ground black pepper to taste

Directions:

1. Melt butter in a saucepan over medium heat.
2. Cook and stir garlic in melted butter until browned, about 5 minutes.
3. Stir turnips into the butter and garlic; cook and stir until just beginning to soften, 7 to 10 minutes.
4. Add cream and Parmesan cheese to the turnip mixture; bring to a simmer and cook, stirring regularly, until the liquid thickens, 10 to 15 minutes.
5. Stir green onion, oregano, parsley, salt, and black pepper into the turnip mixture; cook until the green onion slightly wilts, 1 to 2 minutes.

Butternut Squash and Turnip Soup

Ingredients:

3 tbsps. butter
1 tbsp. olive oil
2 cups cubed butternut squash
2 cups cubed turnips
1 cup thinly sliced celery
1 onion, diced
3 cloves garlic, minced
1 quart chicken stock
1 bay leaf
1 tbsp. honey
¼ tsp. ground black pepper
¼ tsp. ground nutmeg
? tsp. ground coriander
? tsp. cayenne pepper
1 pinch salt to taste

Directions:

1. Heat the butter and olive oil in a skillet over medium heat.
2. Stir in the butternut squash, turnips, celery, onion, and garlic; cook and stir until the vegetables just begin to brown, about 10 minutes.
3. Meanwhile, heat the chicken stock in a large pot over medium heat until simmering.
4. Transfer the vegetables to simmering stock, and add the bay leaf, honey, pepper, nutmeg, coriander, cayenne pepper, and salt. Continue simmering until all the vegetables are softened, about 20 minutes.
5. Remove the bay leaf before serving.

Amish Turnip

Ingredients:

1 cup cooked mashed turnip
1 cup bread crumbs
1 tbsp. sugar
Salt to taste
1 egg, beaten
1 cup milk
1 tbsp. butter

Directions:

1. Mix all the ingredients with half of the bread crumbs.
2. Place in greased casserole.
3. Cover with the rest of the crumbs and bake 45 minutes at 350 degrees.

Turnips In Gravy

Ingredients:

4 whole turnips
3 cans of gravy
1/3 of a stick of low fat butter
1 pinch of sea salt
1-3 pinches of black pepper (you can decide the amount)

Directions:

1. Cut the turnips in half.
2. Boil the turnips on high for about 15-25 minutes. Prepare the gravy.
3. After the turnips are done, lay them down on a plate.
4. Put gravy over and add salt and pepper. This serves eight.
5. If you have more, double the amount of ingredients.

Reserved Turnips

Ingredients:

1/4 cup whole mixed pickle spices
2 qt. vinegar
2 cups sugar
4 qt. cooked turnip slices or chunks

Directions:

1. Tie spices in a cloth bag; boil with sugar and vinegar about 5 minutes.
2. Remove bag; add cooked turnips and bring to a boil.
3. Can in sterilized jars or use fresh after allowing to stand for a few hours.

Southern Turnips

Ingredients:

1 cube vegetable bouillon
1 cup water
3 cups peeled, cubed turnips
¼ cup minced onion
2 cloves garlic, minced
1 pinch salt and black pepper to taste
1?½ tbsps. sour cream
½ cup shredded sharp white Cheddar cheese
1 tsp. chopped fresh parsley for garnish

Directions:

1. Place the vegetable bouillon cube into a saucepan with the water, and bring to a boil over high heat.
2. Cook until the bouillon cube dissolves, about 1 minute.
3. Stir in the turnips, onion, and garlic, return to a boil, and cook the mixture until the turnips are tender, about 10 minutes.
4. Reduce the heat to a simmer, and cook until most of the liquid has been evaporated, 10 to 15 more minutes.
5. Lightly stir in the sour cream to coat the turnips.
6. Sprinkle with salt and pepper, and top with shredded cheddar cheese and parsley.

Mashed Turnips

Ingredients:

1 large turnip, peeled and cubed
3 white potatoes, peeled and cubed
¼ cup milk
3 tbsps. unsalted butter
1 tsp. white sugar
¾ tsp. salt
¼ tsp. pepper

Directions:

1. Preheat oven to 375 degrees F (190 degrees C).
2. Place turnip and potatoes in a large pot with enough water to cover, and bring to a boil.
3. Cook 25 to 30 minutes, until tender.
4. Remove from heat, and drain.
5. Mix milk, 2 tbsps. butter, and sugar with the turnip and potatoes.
6. Season with salt and pepper.
7. Mash until slightly lumpy.
8. Transfer turnip mixture to a small baking dish. Dot with remaining butter.
9. Cover loosely, and bake 15 minutes in the preheated oven.
10. Remove cover, and continue baking about 8 minutes, until lightly browned.

Turnip Bake

Ingredients:

1 large turnip, peeled and cubed
2 tbsps. butter
1 pinch salt and ground black pepper
2 large apples - peeled, cored, and diced
2 tbsps. brown sugar
1 pinch ground cinnamon
Topping:
¼ cup all-purpose flour
¼ cup brown sugar
2 tbsps. butter, softened

Directions:

1. Preheat oven to 350 degrees F (175 degrees C).
2. Grease an 8-inch casserole dish.
3. Place turnip into a large pot and cover with salted water; bring to a boil.
4. Reduce heat to medium-low and simmer until tender, 15 to 20 minutes.
5. Drain and transfer to a bowl.
6. Mash turnip, 2 tbsps. butter, salt, and pepper together until smooth.
7. Toss apples with 2 tbsps. brown sugar and cinnamon in a bowl.
8. Spread half the turnip mixture into the prepared casserole dish; top with half the apples.
9. Repeat with remaining turnip mixture and apple mixture.
10. Mix flour, 1/4 cup brown sugar, and 2 tbsps. softened butter by hand in a bowl until mixture is an evenly coarse meal-texture; sprinkle over casserole.
11. Bake in the preheated oven until cooked through and bubbling, about 1 hour.

Bacon And Turnip Casserole

Ingredients:

12 turnips, peeled & cubed
1/2 lb. bacon, chopped
2 onions, chopped
1 clove garlic, minced
1 med. size green pepper, chopped
2 egg yolks, beaten
1/3 cup evaporated milk
3 slices bread, toasted & crumbled
1/4 cup butter, melted
1 tbsp. chopped green onion with tops
2 tsp. chopped fresh parsley
1/2 tsp. salt
1/4 tsp. pepper

Directions:

1. Place turnips in a large saucepan; cover with water, and bring to a boil.
2. Cover and cook 30 minutes or until turnips are tender.
3. Drain and mash; set aside.
4. Cook bacon in a large skillet until crisp; remove bacon, reserving 2 tbsps. drippings in skillet. Set bacon aside. Saute onion, garlic and green pepper in reserved drippings until tender.
5. Stir turnips and remaining ingredients except bacon. Spoon into a 3 quart casserole; top with reserved bacon.
6. Bake at 350 degrees for 30 minutes. Yield: 8 to 10 servings.

Finnish Turnip Casserole

Ingredients:

3 large carrots, cubed
1 large turnip, cubed
3 tbsps. softened butter
½ tsp. salt
¼ cup all-purpose flour
¼ cup white sugar
2 eggs
½ cup milk
2 tbsps. white sugar
¼ tsp. ground cinnamon

Directions:

1. Preheat an oven to 350 degrees F (175 degrees C).
2. Grease a 2 quart casserole dish.
3. Place the carrot and turnip cubes into a large pot and cover with salted water.
4. Bring to a boil over high heat, then reduce heat to medium-low, cover, and simmer until tender, about 20 minutes.
5. Drain and allow to steam dry for a minute or two.
6. Return the carrots and turnips to the pot, and mash well with the butter, salt, flour and 1/4 cup of sugar.
7. Whisk together the eggs and milk in a bowl, then stir into the mashed carrot mixture until blended.
8. Scrape into the prepared casserole dish.
9. Stir together 2 tbsps. of sugar with the cinnamon in a small bowl, and sprinkle over the top of the carrot mash.
10. Bake in the preheated oven until the carrot mash has slightly firmed and the top has begun to turn golden brown, about 45 minutes.

Buttered Glazed Turnips

Ingredients:

5 med. turnips, peel and slice about 1/4 inch thick
1 beef bouillon cube (or 1 tsp. granulated bouillon)
1/4 cup butter, melted
2 tbsp. brown sugar
Black or red crushed pepper to taste
Salt (if you like) to taste

Directions:

1. Cook turnips until tender in water in which cube is dissolved.
2. Drain and place in casserole dish.
3. Drizzle with melted butter, sprinkle with sugar and pepper.
4. Place in 350 degree oven for about 15 minutes until flavors are blended. Serve hot.

Braised Turnips

Ingredients:

2 lbs. turnips, peeled and cut into 1/2" cubes
1/4 lb. bacon
1/2 cup onion, minced
2 tbsp. unsalted butter
1/2 cup chicken stock
3/4 tsp. sugar
3/4 tsp. salt
2 tbsp. parsley, minced
Juice of 1 lemon

Directions:

1. Blanch the turnips in boiling salty water for 1 minute.
2. Drain the turnips in a colander, refresh them under running cold water, and pat them dry.
3. In a large skillet, saute bacon, diced, until crisp; drain.
4. Add to the skillet onions and butter, and cook until onions are soft.
5. Add the turnips, chicken stock, sugar and salt.
6. Toss the mixture, and braise it, covered, over moderately low heat for 15 minutes or until turnips are tender.
7. Cook the mixture, uncovered, stirring, until the liquid is evaporated.
8. Add bacon, parsley, lemon juice, and salt and pepper to taste.
9. Toss the mixture well, and transfer it to a heated serving dish.

Cheesy Stuffed Turnips

Ingredients:

6 med. turnips, peeled
3/4 cup crushed saltine crackers
1/2 cup shredded Cheddar cheese
1 1/2 cup milk (not used all together)
5 tbsp. butter, melted (not used all together)
Paprika
2 tbsp. all-purpose flour

Directions:

1. Cook turnips, covered, in boiling salted water 25 minutes or until tender. Hollow out each turnip, leaving a 1/2-inch shell. Finely chip turnip centers (should have about 1 cup of chopped turnip).
2. Combine crushed crackers, cheese, 1/4 cup of milk and 3 tbsps. of butter.
3. Fill turnips with cheese mixture.
4. Place in a greased 10 x 6 x 2-inch baking pan. Brush with melted butter; sprinkle with paprika.
5. Bake, covered, in 350 degree oven for 25 minutes. Uncover and bake 10 minutes more.
6. Melt remaining 2 tbsps. butter; blend in flour, 1/4 tsp. salt and 1/8 tsp. pepper.
7. Add remaining milk.
8. Cook and stir until bubbly.
9. Cook 2 minutes more.
10. Stir in chopped turnip.
11. Heat through. Spoon sauce over turnips.

Turnip Soup

Ingredients:

2 tbsp. chopped onion
2 tbsp. butter
2 tbsp. flour
1 qt. hot milk
1 cup grated raw turnips
Salt and pepper to taste

Directions:

1. Saute onion in butter for a few minutes.
2. Blend in flour; add milk gradually, turnips, salt and pepper.
3. Cook stirring frequently, until turnips are tender, about 10 minutes.

Turnip Salad

Ingredients:

4 turnips, peeled and chopped
1 bunch green onions, chopped
2 Granny Smith apples - peeled, cored and chopped
4 slices canned pineapple, chopped
½ cup white sugar
¼ cup vegetable oil
1 tbsp. water
1 tsp. salt
¼ tsp. ground black pepper

Directions:

1. Bring a large pot of salted water to a boil.
2. Add turnips and cook until tender but still firm, about 15 minutes.
3. Drain, and cool.
4. In a large bowl, combine the turnips, green onions, apples, pineapple and sugar.
5. Stir to evenly coat with the sugar.
6. Whisk together the oil, water, salt and pepper.
7. Pour dressing over fruit and vegetables.
8. Toss and refrigerate overnight.

Finnish Turnip Casserole

Ingredients:

2 med. turnips, peeled & diced (about 6 c.)
1/4 cup fine dry bread crumbs
1/2 tsp. nutmeg
1/4 cup cream or milk
1 tsp. salt
1 egg, beaten
3 tbsp. butter
1 tbsp. brown sugar
1/2 tsp. cinnamon

Directions:

1. Cook turnip until soft.
2. Drain and mash. Soak bread crumbs in cream and stir in nutmeg, cinnamon, salt, sugar and beaten egg.
3. Combine with mashed turnip. Turn into a buttered 2 1/2 quart casserole. Dot top with butter, a bit more cinnamon and bread crumbs.
4. Bake at 350 degrees for 10 or until lightly browned on top.

Crispy Turnip Fries

Ingredients:

8 med. turnips
1/4 cup grated Parmesan cheese
1 tsp. onion powder
1 tsp. ground paprika

Directions:

1. Preheat oven to 425 degrees. Spray a large baking sheet with non-stick cooking spray.
2. Peel and cut turnips into 2 1/2 x 1/2 inch sticks. In large Ziplock bag, combine cheese, onion powder, and paprika.
3. Add turnips; seal bag and toss to coat turnips.
4. Place on baking sheet.
5. Bake 15-20 minutes, or until turnips are tender and golden.

Fried Turnips

Ingredients:

3-4 lb. turnip roots
1 lb. bacon
1 cup chopped onions
1 cup chopped green peppers
2 tbsp. sugar

Directions:

1. Cook turnips until tender.
2. Fry bacon until crisp and break into pieces.
3. Pour all of bacon grease off, reserving 2-3 tbsps.. Saute peppers and onions in bacon grease until tender.
4. Add turnips and sugar, mixing well.

Dijon Turnips

Ingredients:

1 bag turnips, peeled and cleaned
1/4 cup softened butter
1 tsp. Dijon mustard
Black pepper to taste

Directions:

1. Preheat oven to 350 degrees.
2. Peel and slice turnips in half.
3. Mix mustard and butter, spread on turnips.
4. Place turnips in shallow baking dish and sprinkle with black pepper.
5. Bake until tender.

Dilled Turnip And Carrot Au Gratin

Ingredients:

3 cup sliced turnips, 1/4 inch thick, about 1 1/4 lb.
1 cup thinly sliced carrots
1 tbsp. butter
1 tbsp. all purpose flour
1 tsp. dried dill weed
1/4 tsp. salt
Dash of pepper
3/4 cup milk
1/2 cup shredded American cheese (2 oz.)
1/3 cup plain croutons, crushed

Directions:

1. Quarter large slices of turnips.
2. In a 2 quart saucepan, cook turnips and carrots, covered, in small amount of boiling salted water 5-7 minutes or until crisp-tender.
3. Drain well.
4. For sauce, in small saucepan melt butter; stir in flour, dill weed, salt, and pepper.
5. Stir in milk.
6. Cook and store until thickened and bubbly.
7. Cook and stir 1-2 minutes more.
8. Stir in cheese until melted. Gently stir in turnips and carrots.
9. Transfer to an ungreased 1 1/2 quart casserole.
10. Sprinkle croutons over top.
11. Bake uncovered in 350 degree oven for 20-25 minutes or until heated through.

Louisiana Style Turnips

Ingredients:

6 med. turnips (peeled and diced)
1 link of smoked sausage (sliced thin)
1 tbsp. onion (chopped)
1 tbsp. shortening
1 pkg. dried shrimp (soaked in hot water 5 min.)
3 tsp. sugar

Directions:

1. Fry sausage and onions in shortening.
2. Add turnips, shrimp, sugar, salt and pepper to taste. Simmer 40 minutes in covered pan.

Mashed Potatoes With Turnips

Ingredients:

2 lg. turnips, peeled and cut into chunks
4 lg. potatoes, peeled and quartered
1/2 cup finely chopped onion
2 tbsp. of butter
3/4 tsp. salt
1/8 tsp. white pepper

Directions:

1. Cook turnips, covered, in small amount of boiling salted water for 10 minutes; add potatoes and onion; and cook until vegetables are tender, 15 or 20 minutes.
2. Drain well.
3. Mash vegetables with butter, salt, and pepper. Serve hot.

Lemon Turnip Sticks

Ingredients:

2 med. turnips, peeled & cut into sticks (about 2 cups)
1 tbsp. butter
2 tsp. parsley, snipped
1 tsp. finely chopped onion
1 tsp. lemon juice
Salt & pepper

Directions:

1. Cook turnip sticks in boiling water until tender, about 20 minutes.
2. Drain; add butter, parsley, onion and lemon juice.
3. Toss to coat.
4. Season to taste.

Turnip Onion Soup

Ingredients:

4 med. white turnips, grated
8 tbsp. butter
8 med. onions, sliced
8 tbsp. flour
6 to 8 cup beef stock
2 cup water, optional
Salt
Freshly ground pepper
8 slices French bread, toasted
1 cup grated Parmesan cheese

Directions:

1. Place grated turnips in a pot covered with water.
2. Bring to boil 1 to 3 minutes.
3. Drain. Dry turnips with paper towel.
4. Melt 4 tbsps. butter in large heavy pan.
5. Add onions and cook over medium heat until rich brown.
6. Add turnips and continue cooking until turnips light brown and onions caramelized to nutty color.
7. Stir in flour, tbsp. at a time. Taste beef stock; if strong or salty use less and dilute with water.
8. Add beef stock and water and stir until boils.
9. Then simmer 30 minutes. Salt and pepper if desired.
10. Sprinkle toasted bread with Parmesan cheese and broil to slightly brown. Ladle soup into bowls over toasted bread or top with bread.

Turnip with Coconut

Ingredients:

2 tbsps. vegetable oil
½ tsp. mustard seed
¼ tsp. asafoetida powder
2 turnips, quartered and sliced thinly
4 eaches fresh turnip leaves, chopped
½ onion, minced
1 tsp. paprika
1 tsp. turmeric
½ tsp. salt
2 tbsps. water
1 tbsp. shredded coconut

Directions:

1. Heat the oil in a skillet over high heat; cook the mustard seeds in the hot oil until the seeds no longer are crackling.
2. Stir the asafoetida powder into the mustard seeds; add the turnips, turnip leaves, and onion to the skillet.
3. Season the mixture with the paprika, turmeric, and salt.
4. Pour the water over the mixture, place a cover on the skillet, reduce heat to medium, and cook until the turnip is cooked yet remains crunchy, 5 to 7 minutes. Return heat to high to cook off any excess water.
5. Mix the coconut into the mixture just before serving.

Potato-Turnip Casserole

Ingredients:

4 med. sized potatoes, peeled
2 med. sized turnips, peeled
3/4 cup evaporated milk
3 tbsp. butter
2 tsp. salt
2 tsp. minced onion
1 tbsp. parsley
1 cup cheddar cheese, shredded

Directions:

1. Boil peeled potatoes and turnips until tender; drain.
2. Stir in milk and butter.
3. Mash.
4. Add remaining ingredients, mixing well.
5. Pour mixture into buttered casserole.
6. Bake at 400 degrees for 30 minutes.

Mashed Turnips And Potatoes

Ingredients:

3 sm. potatoes, peeled & cubed
1 1/2 cup turnips, peeled & cubed
1-2 tbsp. skim milk
2 tbsp. unsalted butter
1 tbsp. fresh chopped parsley
1 tbsp. chopped chives
Dash ground red pepper
2 tbsp. freshly grated Parmesan cheese

Directions:

1. In a large saucepan, over medium heat, cook potatoes and turnips in boiling water for 20 to 30 minutes or until fork tender; drain.
2. In a large bowl combine potatoes, turnips, milk and butter.
3. Mash until fluffy.
4. Stir in parsley, chives and red pepper. Spoon mixture into 1 quart shallow baking dish.
5. Sprinkle with Parmesan cheese. Broil 3" to 4" from heat for 1 to 2 minutes or until lightly brown.

Turnip and Blue Cheese Gratin

Ingredients:

2 cloves garlic, smashed
1 pinch salt and pepper to taste
¾ cup half-and-half cream
2 tsps. dried thyme
1 bay leaf
1 large leek - cleaned, and cut into 1/4 inch thick rounds
2 large turnips, peeled and sliced
1 cup cubed butternut squash
4 large mushrooms, sliced
2 large carrots, sliced
1 tsp. chopped fresh rosemary
½ cup crumbled blue cheese
¼ cup shredded Gruyere cheese

Directions:

1. Preheat the oven to 375 degrees F (190 degrees C). Butter a 2 quart casserole dish, rub with one of the garlic cloves, and sprinkle with a little salt. Set aside.
2. Heat the half-and-half in a small saucepan over medium heat.
3. Add the thyme, bay leaf and both garlic cloves.
4. Remove from the heat just before it boils.
5. Place the leek, turnip, squash, mushrooms and carrots into a large saucepan and fill with about 1 inch of water.
6. Bring to a boil, cover and steam over medium heat for about 5 minutes.
7. Drain and layer vegetables into the prepared casserole dish.
8. Sprinkle rosemary in between the layers.
9. Season with salt and pepper and sprinkle blue cheese and Gruyere cheese over the top. Strain the half-and-half and pour into the casserole.
10. Bake, uncovered, in the preheated oven until vegetables are tender and sauce is thick, about 40 minutes. Uncover for the last 20 minutes to allow the top to brown.

Stir Fried Cabbage And Turnips

Ingredients:

1 1/2 tbsp. olive oil
2 cup coarsely chopped cabbage
1/2 lb. turnips, cut into 1/4" cubes
1/4 tsp. ground cumin

Directions:

1. In a heavy skillet heat the oil over moderately high heat until it is hot but not smoking and in it cook the cabbage and the turnips with the cumin and salt & pepper to taste over moderate heat, stirring for 7-9 minutes or until the vegetables are just tender.

Southern Turnips

Ingredients:

2 lbs. turnips, peeled & cubed
2 med. size new potatoes, unpeeled & cubed
1 bay leaf
4 cup water
1 med. onion, chopped
2 tbsp. bacon drippings
1/2 tsp. salt
1/2 tsp. pepper
1/8 tsp. red pepper
2 tbsp. minced fresh parsley (opt.)

Directions:

1. Combine first 4 ingredients in a Dutch oven.
2. Bring to a boil, cover, reduce heat and simmer 20 minutes or until vegetables are tender.
3. Drain; remove bay leaf. Saute onion in bacon drippings until tender.
4. Add turnips, potatoes, salt, pepper and red pepper; toss gently. Serve. Eat and enjoy!

Scalloped Turnips And Apples

Ingredients:

4 cup sliced cooked turnips
2 cup sliced raw apples
1/2 cup brown sugar
1 tsp. salt
1/4 cup butter
1/4 cup buttered bread crumbs

Directions:

1. Arrange 2 cups turnips in bottom of greased casserole and cover with 1 cup apples.
2. Sprinkle with half the sugar, salt and dot with half the butter, repeat the layers.
3. Cover and bake at 350 degrees until apples are almost tender (20-30 minutes). Uncover and sprinkle with buttered crumbs.
4. Bake until apples are tender and crumbs are lightly browned.

Stewed Turnips

Ingredients:

8 to 10 turnips
1 lg. onion, chopped
1 tsp. garlic
1 tsp. parsley
Salt & pepper to taste
1 tbsp. butter

Directions:

1. Boil peeled and cubed turnips until tender. Saute onions in butter until clear.
2. Add garlic, parsley and drained turnips.
3. Cook until soft.

Stuffed Turnips

Ingredients:

6 lg. white turnips (2 lb.)
Boiling water
Salt
1/4 cup butter
1 cup chopped broccoli, fresh or frozen
1/4 lb. mushrooms, washed and chopped
1 clove garlic, crushed
1/2 cup chicken broth
2 tbsp. chopped parsley

Directions:

1. Wash and pare turnips.
2. Cut thin slice off root and stem ends. In 1 inch boiling salted water in large saucepan, cook turnips 20 to 25 minutes, or just until tender; drain and cool slightly. With a spoon, scoop out centers, leaving 1/2 inch shell. Finely chop centers; reserve.
3. Preheat oven to 350 degrees. Butter a 1 1/2 quart baking dish.
4. In hot butter in 10 inch skillet, over medium heat, saute broccoli, mushrooms, garlic and 1/2 tsp. salt, stirring about 5 minutes.
5. Remove from heat, add chopped turnip.
6. Mix well.
7. Spoon into shells, dividing evenly.
8. Place in buttered baking dish.
9. Pour chicken broth around turnips.
10. Bake, covered with foil for 20 to 25 minutes or until hot.
11. Remove from oven, sprinkle with parsley.

Turnip and Apple Bake

Ingredients:

1 turnip
1 tbsp. butter
1 1/2 cup sliced apples
1/4 cup brown sugar
Pinch of cinnamon
Peel, dice and cook turnip.
Drain and mash with 1 tbsp. of butter.
Toss apples with brown sugar and cinnamon.
Arrange layers of apples and turnip in 2 quart greased, casserole,
beginning and ending with turnip.

Topping Ingredients:

1/3 cup flour
1/3 cup brown sugar
2 tbsp. butter

Directions:

1. Mix together until crumbly; sprinkle on top.
2. Bake at 350 degrees for 1 hour.

Turnip and Onion Relish

Ingredients:

5 cup shredded white turnip
2 cup chopped onion
4 tsp. salt
4 cup sugar
3 cup white vinegar
3/4 tsp. paprika
1 tsp. yellow food coloring

Directions:

1. Combine turnip, onion and salt and let stand for 1 hour.
2. Drain.
3. Combine sugar, vinegar, paprika and food color and bring to a boil.
4. Add drained turnip mixture and simmer for 1 minute. Ladle into hot, sterilized jars and seal. Process in boiling water bath for 5 minutes.

Turnip Pickles

Ingredients:

2 lb. sm. white turnips
Celery leaves
Sliced raw beet or beet juice
3 1/2 cup water
1 1/4 cup vinegar
6 or 7 tbsp. salt
2-4 garlic cloves (optional)

Directions:

1. Wash and pare turnips, slicing to fit the appropriate jar.
   Pack with celery leaves, garlic and beet slices, if used.
   Dissolve salt in water, add vinegar and fill jars. Pickles
   ready in about 7-10 days.

Turnip Slaw

Ingredients:

1/4 cup chopped red peppers
1/4 cup sliced green onions
1/4 cup mayonnaise
1 tbsp. vinegar
2 tbsp. sugar
1/4 tsp. salt
1/4 tsp. pepper
4 cup shredded turnips

Directions:

1. In a bowl combine all ingredients, except turnips.
2. Pour over turnips. Refrigerate several hours.

Turnip Soup

Ingredients:

1 qt. milk
2 tbsp. minced onion
2 cup finely grated white turnip, not packed down (pulp and juice)
1 tsp. salt
2 tbsp. butter, blended with 1 tbsp. flour
White pepper to taste
Minced parsley

Directions:

1. Heat milk; add onion, turnip and salt; simmer, covered, for 10 minutes.
2. Add butter-flour mixture; cook and stir constantly over moderately low heat until slightly thickened and bubbly.
3. Stir in pepper and sprinkle with parsley.
4. Makes almost 1 1/2 quarts.

Potato Turnip Pancakes

Ingredients:

2 cup mashed potatoes
1 cup mashed turnips
1/2 cup mashed carrots
1/2 cup chopped celery
1/2 cup chopped onion
2 eggs, unbeaten
6 tbsp. flour
Salt and pepper to taste
1/2 cup mayonnaise
1 (7 oz.) can of tuna, include the fluid from the can of tuna
1 cup corn flakes

Directions:

1. Mix all ingredients well, then drop mixture from tbsp. into skillet containing hot fat. Flatten each cake with back of tbsp., or flour hands, then make into cakes.
2. Fry to a deep, golden brown on each side.

Carrot-Turnip Salad

Ingredients:

1 1/2 cup shredded peeled carrots
1 1/2 cup shredded peeled white turnips
1/2 cup diced green pepper
1/3 cup prepared Good Seasons Zesty Italian salad dressing
Salad greens or pepper rings

Directions:

1. Combine carrots, green pepper and salad dressing in bowl; toss together lightly. Serve on salad greens or green pepper rings.

Turnip Kraut

Ingredients:

1 gallon shredded turnips
4 tbsp. mustard seed
1 1/2 cup white vinegar
3 cup sugar
2 1/2 oz. horseradish
Salt to taste

Directions:

1. Mix all ingredients by hand.
2. Let stand 1 week in refrigerator. Will keep for several months.

Turnips and Onions

Ingredients:

2 tbsps. butter
1 tbsp. olive oil
2 medium turnips, peeled and grated
1 large onion, sliced into rings
1 pinch salt and pepper to taste

Directions:

1. Melt butter with olive oil in a skillet over medium heat.
2. Add the onions, and cook until caramelized, 10 to 15 minutes.
3. Transfer the onion to a bowl, and mix with the grated turnip.
4. Season with salt and pepper. Refrigerate for 30 minutes to allow the flavors to mingle. Serve on small toast or crackers.

Turnip and Blue Cheese Gratin

Ingredients:

2 cloves garlic, smashed
1 pinch salt and pepper to taste
¾ cup half-and-half cream
2 tsps. dried thyme
1 bay leaf
1 large leek - cleaned, and cut into 1/4 inch thick rounds
2 large turnips, peeled and sliced
1 cup cubed butternut squash
4 large mushrooms, sliced
2 large carrots, sliced
1 tsp. chopped fresh rosemary
½ cup crumbled blue cheese
¼ cup shredded Gruyere cheese

Directions:

1. Preheat the oven to 375 degrees F (190 degrees C). Butter a 2 quart casserole dish, rub with one of the garlic cloves, and sprinkle with a little salt. Set aside.
2. Heat the half-and-half in a small saucepan over medium heat.
3. Add the thyme, bay leaf and both garlic cloves.
4. Remove from the heat just before it boils.
5. Place the leek, turnip, squash, mushrooms and carrots into a large saucepan and fill with about 1 inch of water.
6. Bring to a boil, cover and steam over medium heat for about 5 minutes.
7. Drain and layer vegetables into the prepared casserole dish.
8. Sprinkle rosemary in between the layers.
9. Season with salt and pepper and sprinkle blue cheese and Gruyere cheese over the top. Strain the half-and-half and pour into the casserole.
10. Bake, uncovered, in the preheated oven until vegetables are tender and sauce is thick, about 40 minutes. Uncover for the last 20 minutes to allow the top to brown.

Cauliflower and Turnip Salad

Ingredients:

1 pound turnips, cut into bite-sized pieces
2 tbsps. extra-virgin olive oil, divided
1 pound cauliflower florets
½ cup mayonnaise
2 tbsps. prepared yellow mustard
1 tbsp. white vinegar
1 ½ tsps. garlic salt
1 sprig fresh dill, chopped, or to taste
1 pinch black pepper to taste
5 eaches hard-boiled eggs, diced
½ cup chopped onion

Directions:

1. Preheat the oven to 375 degrees F (190 degrees C).
2. Combine turnips and 1 tbsp. olive oil in a bowl and toss.
3. Transfer to a baking sheet in a single layer.
4. Roast in the preheated oven until browned and crisp, 30 to 35 minutes.
5. Combine cauliflower and remaining 1 tbsp. olive oil in a bowl and toss.
6. Transfer to a baking sheet in a single layer.
7. Roast in the hot oven until lightly browned on all sides, 20 to 25 minutes.
8. Mix mayonnaise, mustard, vinegar, garlic salt, fresh dill, and black pepper together in large bowl.
9. Toss roasted turnips and cauliflower, eggs, and onion into the sauce. Refrigerate before serving, about 20 minutes.

Parmesan Crusted Crushed Turnips

Ingredients:

12 small to medium turnips, peeled
Salt
2 tbsps. olive oil
3 cloves garlic, minced
Freshly ground black pepper
1 cup freshly grated Parmesan cheese (or as needed)

Directions:

1. Place peeled turnips in a pot of salted water to cover.
2. Bring to a boil.
3. Cook 20 to 30 minutes or until turnips can be pierced easily with a paring knife.
4. Drain.
5. Let cool slightly.
6. Preheat oven to 375 degrees.
7. Place the turnips on a clean kitchen towel or double layer of paper towels. Gently press each one down until it's approximately 1/2-inch high.
8. Let them drain for 15 minutes then carefully flip them over onto a dry section of the towel or onto fresh paper towels so the other side drains and dries a bit.
9. Combine garlic, olive oil and salt and black pepper, to taste in a small bowl.
10. Line a baking sheet with parchment paper or nonstick aluminum foil.
11. Place the flattened turnips on the lined baking sheet. Brush each turnip with a little of the olive oil and garlic combination.
12. Sprinkle Parmesan cheese over each turnip, gently pressing it down.
13. Carefully and quickly flip each turnip over.
14. Repeat with the remaining olive oil and garlic combination and cheese.
15. Bake for 20 to 25 minutes. Flip each turnip and bake an additional 15 minutes. Garnish with chopped fresh chives and serve.

Tandoori Roasted Turnip Stew

Ingredients:

4 cups chopped turnips turnip
2 shallots, halved
4 tsps. vegetable oil
1 clove garlic, chopped
1 pinch salt
1 pinch freshly ground pepper
1 ½ cups chopped zucchini (1-inch chunks)
1 cup cherry tomatoes, halved
½ (15 oz.) can lentils, drained and rinsed
1 packet Patak's Tandoori Sauce for Two
½ cup cooked quinoa
1 tbsp. finely chopped fresh mint

Directions:

1. Preheat oven to 400 degrees F (204 degrees C).
2. Toss root vegetables with shallots, oil, garlic, salt, and pepper.
3. Place in a 9x9-inch baking dish.
4. Roast, turning occasionally, for 25 to 30 minutes or until vegetables are lightly golden and tender crisp.
5. Stir in zucchini and scatter cherry tomatoes over top; roast for 12 to 15 minutes or until all vegetables are tender.
6. Stir in lentils, Patak's Tandoori Sauce, and quinoa.
7. Cover tightly with foil.
8. Cook, covered, stirring occasionally, for 10 to 15 minutes or until mixture has simmered and heated through.
9. Garnish with mint.

Turnip Crisps

Ingredients:

1 quart peanut oil for frying, or as needed
1 large beet, peeled and sliced paper-thin
1 large sweet potato, peeled and sliced paper-thin
1 turnip, peeled and sliced paper-thin
1 parsnip, peeled and sliced paper-thin
1 golden beet, peeled and sliced paper-thin
1 pinch sea salt to taste
1 pinch freshly cracked black pepper to taste
1 tbsp. malt vinegar, or to taste
1 cup plain Greek yogurt
¼ cup chopped fresh parsley
1 tbsp. chopped fresh mint
1 clove garlic, finely minced
4 eaches green onions, finely chopped
2 tbsps. lemon juice, or to taste
1 pinch salt and ground white pepper to taste

Directions:

1. Heat oil in a deep-fryer or large saucepan to 360 degrees F (182 degrees C).
2. Carefully fry beet, sweet potato, turnip, parsnip, and golden beet slices in the hot oil, working in batches, until golden brown, 2 to 4 minutes.
3. Remove vegetable chips with a slotted spoon and transfer to paper towels to drain. Allow to dry and cool.
4. Season chips with sea salt, cracked black pepper, and malt vinegar to taste.
5. Combine yogurt, parsley, mint, garlic, and green onions together in a bowl.
6. Stir lemon juice, salt, and white pepper into yogurt mixture to your taste preference.

About the Author

Laura Sommers is **The Recipe Lady!**

She is a loving wife and mother who lives on a small farm in Baltimore County, Maryland and has a passion for all things domestic especially when it comes to saving money. She has a profitable eBay business and is a couponing addict. Follow her tips and tricks to learn how to make delicious meals on a budget, save money or to learn the latest life hack!

Visit her Amazon Author Page to see her latest books:

amazon.com/author/laurasommers

Follow the Recipe Lady on **Pinterest**:

http://pinterest.com/therecipelady1

Follow her on Facebook:

https://www.facebook.com/therecipegirl/

Please leave a review:

It's proven that generosity makes you a happier person. So if you are generous enough to leave me a review for this cookbook, then thank you. It has really helped me and my family a lot. I hope that this book has enriched your life.

Other Books by Laura Sommers

Irish Recipes for St. Patrick's Day

Winter Butternut Squash Recipes

Sweet Potato Recipes

Potato Recipes

Recipe Hacks for Mashed Potatoes

Printed in Great Britain
by Amazon